DARING ESCAPE FROM ALCATRAZ

by Matt Chandler

CAPSTONE PRESS
a capstone imprint

Published by Capstone Press, an imprint of Capstone
1710 Roe Crest Drive, North Mankato, Minnesota 56003
capstonepub.com

Library of Congress Cataloging-in-Publication Data
Names: Chandler, Matt, author.
Title: Daring escape from Alcatraz / by Matt Chandler.
Description: North Mankato, Minnesota : Capstone Press, an imprint of Capstone, [2022] | Includes bibliographical references and index. | Audience: Ages 8-11 | Audience: Grades 4-6 | Summary: "Located on an island in San Francisco Bay, Alcatraz was once considered one of the country's most secure prisons. But that didn't stop three prisoners from making a daring escape the night of June 11, 1962. They set sail across the bay on a homemade raft made of raincoats. Then they vanished. What happened to them? Explore the theories and discover why their escape has become one of history's greatest mysteries"-- Provided by publisher.
Identifiers: LCCN 2021023332 (print) | LCCN 2021023333 (ebook) | ISBN 9781663958747 (hardcover) | ISBN 9781666320572 (paperback) | ISBN 9781666320589 (pdf) | ISBN 9781666320602 (kindle edition)
Subjects: LCSH: United States Penitentiary, Alcatraz Island, California--Juvenile literature. | Escaped prisoners--California--Alcatraz Island--Case studies--Juvenile literature. | Escapes--California--Alcatraz Island--Case studies--Juvenile literature.
Classification: LCC HV9474.A4 C54 2022 (print) | LCC HV9474.A4 (ebook) | DDC 365/.641097946--dc23
LC record available at https://lccn.loc.gov/2021023332
LC ebook record available at https://lccn.loc.gov/2021023333

Editorial Credits
Editor: Carrie Sheely; Designer: Kim Pfeffer; Media Researcher: Morgan Walters; Production Specialist: Laura Manthe

Image Credits
Associated Press: Eric Risberg, 7, N-CB, 28, The Dothan Eagle, 23; Newscom: Everett Collection, top 15, Ferrari/ZUMA Press, bottom 9, top 25, bottom 25; Shutterstock: Arne Beruldsen, bottom 15, brian takes photos, 27, Da-ga, bottom 11, Everett Collection, top 11, Jose Carlos Castro Antelo, Cover, Milan Rademakers, 21, Nickolay Stanev, 19, Rolf_52, top 9, T.W., 5, Xavier Hoenner, 17; Wikimedia: United States National Archives at San Francisco, 13

Source Notes
Page 16, "They ended up at . . ." "Dutch Scientists Claim to Have Solved Mystery of 1962 Alcatraz Prisoner Escape," *KPIX 5*, December 15, 2014, https://sanfrancisco.cbslocal.com/2014/12/15/dutch-scientists-claim-to-have-solved-mystery-of-1962-alcatraz-prisoner-escape/
Page 24, "If You Announce . . . " "Alcatraz Escape: Fugitive John Anglin's Name on Letter to Police," *BBC News*, January 25, 2018, https://www.bbc.com/news/world-us-canada-42826582

All internet sites appearing in back matter were available and accurate when this book was sent to press.

Table of Contents

Words in **bold** are in the glossary.

INTRODUCTION

Escape from the Rock

The lights were out in Alcatraz prison. It was late in the evening of June 11, 1962. Prisoners Frank Morris and brothers Clarence and John Anglin slipped from their prison cots. The men squeezed through vents in their cells. For months they had been preparing for this moment. In the hall behind the cell block they gathered the raft, paddles, and life jackets they had secretly made. The men carried their supplies to the roof of the prison. In the dark, they climbed down a pipe 50 feet (15 meters) to the ground. If the guards spotted them, they could be shot and killed. They ran for the shore. The prisoners jumped into their raft and paddled into the darkness of San Francisco Bay. The men had escaped the prison nicknamed "The Rock"! It was considered the most secure prison in the United States.

Alcatraz prison sits on Alcatraz Island, which is surrounded by San Francisco Bay.

Fact

Frank Morris planned much of the escape. He was highly intelligent with an IQ of 133. An average score is about 100.

CHAPTER 1

The Big Plan

Frank Morris, John Anglin, and Clarence Anglin were all **convicted** bank robbers. The Anglin brothers met Morris when all three were in federal prison in Atlanta, Georgia. Each man had tried to escape from prison in the past. It was their escape attempts that got them sent to Alcatraz. Because the prison sat on an island in the middle of San Francisco Bay, it was widely believed to be impossible to escape.

Once they arrived in Alcatraz, the three men received cells close to each other. That made it easy to begin to plan their escape. Thirty-one men had tried to escape Alcatraz before them. Nearly all were caught or killed. But these failed attempts didn't stop Morris and the Anglin brothers from trying. In December 1961, the men began to plan their escape.

Fact

Morris and the Anglin brothers had an **accomplice.** Allen West planned the escape with the other men. But West couldn't fit through the hole in his cell wall. The other prisoners left without him.

A 2007 exhibit about the 1962 prison escape shows Frank Morris (left), Clarence Anglin (middle), and John Anglin (right).

Preparing to Escape Alcatraz

Each cell in Alcatraz had an air vent. The men dug out the vents to create holes to crawl through. That led them to an unguarded hallway. The convicts set up a secret work area in the space above their cells. Each night they met there to build the tools needed for their escape. They collected more than 50 raincoats to create a raft and life vests. They cut and sewed the raincoats into a raft. They used the hot pipes in the prison to seal the seams shut and make the raft airtight. They collected wood to make paddles. The prisoners even created fake heads to put in their beds to make it appear they were asleep when the guards came to check on prisoners.

A cell of one of the escapees shows the hole dug out of the wall below the sink.

HEADS UP

The fake heads the men created were one of the most important parts of their escape plan. Guards did a head count every night to make sure all prisoners were in their cells. The prisoners created their fake heads by mixing together toilet paper, cardboard, and cement chips. They shaped the paste into heads that hardened. The men collected human hair from the prison barbershop to make their heads look more realistic.

The dummy heads made by Morris, the Anglin brothers, and Allen West

Challenges to Surviving

For months the prisoners worked on their escape plans without getting caught. But their planning wasn't perfect. The men had to paddle 1.25 miles (2 kilometers) to land. The paddles they made were short and may not have been strong enough to withstand the rough **currents** of the bay. There is also a question of whether the raft was strong enough to hold the weight of three men. Morris and the Anglin brothers weighed about 440 pounds (199 kilograms) together. Part of the raft was discovered the next day washed up on Angel Island. Was that **proof** the raft failed, and the men drowned? Or could the men have made it to land and lived? What happened to them remains a great mystery.

To get to San Francisco (background) from Alcatraz, the escapees would have had to survive the bay's cold waters and strong currents.

Fact

The men used metal spoons to dig out the holes in their cells to escape. Each night Frank Morris played his accordion to hide the sound of the digging from the guards.

CHAPTER 2

A Watery Grave

The bodies of the prisoners were never found. The most common **theory** is that the men drowned. The water was very cold. The raft would almost certainly have taken on water. Experts point to the raft supposedly discovered near Angel Island following the escape. If the men lost their raft, would they have been able to still reach land? Many people say the prisoners could not have survived the cold water. But that may not be true. Six months later, another inmate escaped The Rock. John Paul Scott swam all the way to San Francisco. The water was much colder than in June.

In 1962, John Paul Scott escaped from The Rock and swam to San Francisco. He was found ashore unconscious and near death.

Police Cover-Up?

Alcatraz was said to be inescapable. If three men truly escaped, it would make the authorities seem like they weren't doing their jobs well. Some people say that is why law enforcement quickly said the men drowned. They might have wanted the public to believe the prisoners had died. The authorities said the men planned to steal a car once they reached land. The Federal Bureau of Investigation (FBI) said no cars were stolen during the time of the escape. But there is a report a car was stolen. The report was made shortly after the escape, but it wasn't revealed to the public until years later. Did police cover up this fact and others?

When the prisoners' escape was discovered, many people began questioning whether Alcatraz was as secure as authorities said it was.

Fact

Prisoners in Alcatraz enjoyed very warm showers. The prison officials didn't want the men to get comfortable with cold water and make an escape easier.

Showers at Alcatraz prison

CHAPTER 3

The Possibility of Survival

The strongest proof the men survived may have come from a group of Dutch scientists. In 2014, they used computer models to re-create the escape. The scientists used the exact weather, the currents, and **tides** at the time of the 1962 escape. They determined it was possible that the prisoners made it safely to land. "They ended up at the north shore of the Golden Gate Bridge, near Horseshoe Bay," Dutch scientist Rolf Hut said.

According to one study, the prisoners would have ended up in Horseshoe Bay near the Golden Gate Bridge.

The Science of Currents

Imagine if you just escaped Alcatraz and made it to land. You don't need the raft, life jackets, or paddles anymore. You just want to get away fast! The prisoners would have left those items at the water's edge and continued their escape.

The Dutch scientists used their computer model to explain how the items could have gotten from the Golden Gate Bridge to Angel Island. They say the rough and fast-moving water would have carried the **evidence** back toward Angel Island. The police used the evidence on Angel Island as proof the men drowned. The Dutch scientists say it could be proof the men survived. The current could have carried it back away from where the prisoners came ashore.

Angel Island (back) is about 2 miles (3.2 km) north of Alcatraz Island (front).

BUSTING THE MYTH

In 2003, the TV show *MythBusters* re-created the escape. The show's stars made rafts from raincoats. They made homemade paddles. They left at the same time in the same weather as the Alcatraz prisoners. They even wore the same type of clothes the prisoners would have worn. Less than one hour after they left Alcatraz Island, the men reached the shore in San Francisco. They proved it is possible the convicts survived the escape.

The White Boat

Most people who believe the men died point to the science behind cold water. The water was 54 degrees Fahrenheit (12.2 degrees Celsius) the night of the escape. In cold water, a condition called **hypothermia** can set in. The men could have died from the exposure in as little as one hour. But what if the men weren't in the water for long? In 2016, a man claimed he and an accomplice helped the prisoners escape. He said he drove a white boat into the bay and picked up Morris and the Anglin brothers. The man claimed he took them to shore and helped them flee. They headed north to Seattle, Washington.

The man said he and the accomplice had a fight with the convicts. He said they murdered the prisoners and buried their bodies near a highway. Police searched the area the man claimed to have buried the bodies. They found nothing. It seems possible the story was just a **hoax**.

Some people think the prisoners might have escaped after someone picked them up in a boat.

CHAPTER 4

Proof of Life?

Did the Anglin brothers survive and send their mother cards and gifts after they escaped Alcatraz? Many people believe they did. They say it is proof at least two of the prisoners survived.

David Widner is John and Clarence Anglin's nephew. He told CBS News their grandmother Rachel received roses with cards signed by John and Clarence for years after the escape. Widner also gave investigators a Christmas card signed by the Anglin brothers he said was sent after the escape.

Former U.S. Marshal Art Roderick said the handwriting on the card was proven to belong to one of the Anglin brothers. But authorities were not certain the year the card was sent. **Skeptics** say it was sent before the escape.

David Widner's mother, Marie, posed with newspaper articles and family photos of her two brothers in 2013.

Fact

One report claims the Anglin brothers even disguised themselves and attended their mom's funeral in 1973.

The Anglin Letter

In 2013, a letter was sent to the San Francisco police. The writer claimed to be John Anglin. ". . . If you announce on TV that I will be promised to first go to jail for no more than a year and get medical attention, I will write back to let you know exactly where I am. . . ." the letter said. Anglin said in the letter that he was suffering from cancer.

The U.S. Marshals Service compared the handwriting to samples from John Anglin. The results were **inconclusive**.

Photo Evidence

In the early 1990s, a childhood friend of the Anglin brothers gave their family a photo. He claimed it was a photo of John and Clarence in Brazil. The man's name was Fred Brizzi. He said the brothers were living on a farm. Experts used facial recognition software to analyze the photo. They claim the software proved the photo was of the Anglin brothers.

Facial recognition software compared images of John and Clarence to the photo that was supposedly of the brothers in Brazil.

CLARENCE ANGLIN, DOB 5-11-31, age 31, Ht- 5'11½", Wt- 168 lbs., build medium, eyes hazel, comp. light, tattoo: "Zona" left wrist; "Nita" right 4 arm.

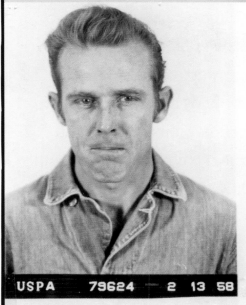

USPA 79624 2 13 58

John William Anglin, FBI #4 745 119

CHAPTER 5

Clues from the Clock

The Dutch study suggests that the difference between life and death for the prisoners could have been a matter of minutes. Between 11:00 p.m. and midnight, the current could have carried them to land in San Francisco. If they left earlier or later, they would likely have been swept out to sea and drowned. They were in their beds at 9:30 p.m. when guards checked. The authorities claimed they left immediately after that count. That could mean they left the island near 10:00. If that's the case, the Dutch study suggests they would have drowned. If they stayed in their cells a bit longer, they may have survived.

Whether the escapees lived or died could depend on how long they waited inside their cells.

Dead or Alive?

If they are alive today, Frank Morris and the Anglin brothers are all in their 90s. The U.S. Marshals Service continues to investigate all leads. The agency says it will keep the case active until the men are proven dead or until each man turns 99 years old.

The truth may never be known. What do you think happened to the escapees?

Crews on a Coast Guard helicopter and boat searched for the prisoners on June 12, 1962.

The Main Theories

1. The men drowned.

The water was a chilly 54°F (12.2°C) the night the men escaped. Many people believe it was too difficult for the three convicts to get to shore.

2. The men paddled to San Francisco and landed near the Golden Gate Bridge.

The current in the water that night could have carried the men toward the Golden Gate Bridge. In 2003, the TV show *MythBusters* re-created the escape. The stars of the show built a raft and paddled it to San Francisco, easily surviving the waters.

3. The men survived, and the Anglin brothers moved to South America.

In the 1990s, a former friend of the Anglin brothers gave their family a photo. He said it was taken in 1975 in Brazil. The man claimed it was the brothers. An analyst said the photo is very likely of the two escapees.

4. The men were picked up by a boat, taken to land, and later murdered.

More than 50 years after the escape, a dying man claimed he helped the convicts escape. The man confessed to picking up the escapees in a boat. The man claims he murdered the prisoners and buried their bodies. But many people believe the man's claims are untrue.

Glossary

accomplice (uh-KOMP-plus)—someone who is working with another in wrongdoing

convicted (kuhm-VIKT-ed)—to be found guilty of a crime

current (KUHR-uhnt)—the movement of water in a river or an ocean

evidence (EV-uh-duhnss)—information, items, and facts that help prove something to be true or false

hoax (HOHKS)—a trick to make people believe something that is not true

hypothermia (hye-puh-THUR-mee-uh)—a life-threatening condition that occurs when a person's body temperature falls several degrees below normal

inconclusive (in-kun-KLU-siv)—leading to no conclusion or certain result

proof (PROOF)—facts or evidence that something is true

skeptic (SKEP-tik)—a person who questions things that other people believe in

theory (THEE-ur-ee)—an idea that explains something that is unknown

tide (TIDE)—the constant change in sea level that is caused by the pull of the sun and the moon on the earth

Read More

Braun, Eric. *Could You Escape Alcatraz?: An Interactive Survival Adventure.* North Mankato, MN: Capstone, 2020.

Chandler, Matt. *Alcatraz: A Chilling Interactive Adventure.* North Mankato, MN: Capstone, 2017.

Sullivan, Tom. *Jailbreak at Alcatraz.* New York: Balzer and Bray, 2021.

Internet Sites

FBI: Alcatraz Escape
fbi.gov/history/famous-cases/alcatraz-escape

National Park Service: Alcatraz Island
nps.gov/alca/index.htm

Was the Escape from Alcatraz Successful?
history.com/news/alcatraz-escape-new-evidence-anglin-brothers

Index

Author Biography

Matt Chandler is the author of more than 65 books for children, including *Side-by-Side Baseball Stars*, which won the 2015 Outstanding Children's Book Award from the American Society of Journalists and Authors. Matt lives in New York with his wife, Amber, and his children, Zoey and Ollie.